EDEN

HUMANITY
WHEAT OR WEEDS

NITORIC JENKINS

WHEAT ~OR~ WEEDS

My insight and the empowerment from God, fortunately, will not allow me to accept the adverse outcome of what the unwarranted and disproportionate surroundings have concluded. Located here in this societal cerebral chokehold that is continuously trying to restrict growth, all while trying to throttle the very diverse essence of Humanity.

> *Numerous of times I've came across people who were not willing to remove their limited thinking, so I too could obtain a fair opportunity in the pursuit of happiness. Nevertheless, haters I still made it and those limitations that choked like an insecticide smoke bomb, poisoning the air, did not win. Excuse me; I'm trying to <u>BREATHE</u>.*
>
> ~Nitoric R. Jenkins~

Copyright 2016 © by Nitoric Jenkins

All rights reserved. This book is protected by the copyright laws of the United States of America, and beyond. This book may not be copied or reprinted for commercial gain or profit. The use of short quotations or occasional page copying for personal or group study is permitted. Permission will be granted upon request. Unless otherwise identified, Scripture quotations are taken from the King James Version. Copyright © 1984 by Thomas Nelson. Used by permission. All rights reserved.

Eden Botched Humanity
PO BOX 920614
Houston, Texas 77292

This book is available on Amazon, Barnes&Noble, Edenbotchedhumanity.com and Retail Distribution Worldwide. Also, available in eBook format, Audio and Hard Cover. Readers if you enjoy my work, please click the donate button on my website and help support upcoming work, Thanks.

Reach us online at: www.edenbotchedhumanity.com

Library of Congress Cataloging-in-Publication Data is available.

ISBN- 13: 978-0-692-06372-9 Hardcover
ISBN- 13: 978-0-692-96793-5 Paperback

For Worldwide Distribution, Printed in the U.S.A.

I Nitoric R. Jenkins, simply want to say
GOD Thank You
Lord JESUS Thank You

*Rethinking
"My Direction"*

After going through so many struggles just trying to survive, everything became operational, and I stop enjoying life. One day while driving my car, I asked God, why am I not happy, why am I not enjoying life, now that the storm's over? God whispered, "Nitoric, because you are still in survival mode." Let go and live.

Do not let broken
Limited thinking People
Hold back progression

Nor
Let their standards impede your growth

*In this season
God is now separating
Wheat from the Tare.*

*Did Eden Fail Humanity?
Let's Take a Look*

CONTENTS

PART 1
Appetizer

Chapter 1
Innocent | 7

Chapter 2
Faith Becoming Real for Real | 19

Chapter 3
Homeless | 39

Chapter 4
Trying to Make Sense of Things of GOD | 53

Chapter 5
Let's Break Bread | 65

PART 2
Stop Trying To Copy God: It Never Ends Well

Chapter 6
KNOW WHO YOU SERVE | 87

Author's Thoughts | 111
About the Author | 113
Acknowledgements | 118
Grandmother Helen | 123

Eden Botched Humanity Wheat or Weeds look at Humanity from a different Paradigm. A Correlation Analysis used by demonstrating a relationship between the Garden of Eden's errors and how over the centuries Humanity still today are dealing with hostile forces that keep Humanity from reaching full restoration more so in the United States.

Humility is one of many common themes established within the book, for such a politically charged climate now faced. The Political events occurred has now positioned our Nation to look closer at the urgency of this alarming change. Above all, male or female please remember that we have the power to create No, against anything that tries to take the Humility out of being Human toward one another. Finding Faith, Hope, and Healing in the 21st Century.

Eden Botched Humanity Wheat or Weeds bring forth awareness and addresses concerns about Urban Planning and Infrastructure Management misrepresentation across the board in urban cities here in America. Data that describes there are no real intentions today for this generation to overcome poverty barriers. The book expresses the Political propaganda governed by demonic influences and Leadership that keep Humanity divided.

APPETIZER

"Please understand that having an ability to make does not always mean permission to create."

~Nitoric Jenkins~

The making of Adam and Eve was Not Authorized by God to replicate humans. God had already created males and females and instructed them to be productive and increase. Adam and Eve are not the first people created, and they are not the first family. God created Humans and sent them out into the <u>earth</u> to live life abundantly.

Readers watch carefully, Adam and Eve had two sons named Cain and Abel. Over time Cain became envious of his brother Abel and killed him. As part of Cain's punishment for committing murder, Cain could no longer live with his family and was cast out to the east of Eden, and there is where Cain met his wife, in a place called <u>Nod</u>, (See Genesis 4:16,17 KJV).

Many believe that Adam and Eve were the first Humans created, and of course, everyone entitled to their beliefs. Meanwhile, since Eve gave birth to Cain and Abel, please explain the existed people who lived in Nod?

Scholars, Cain found his wife outside the garden, and that means lives lived before and during the making of Adam or an Eve.

Observe when limitations placed on God, He can be found in another location doing a new thing. (See Genesis 4:16). In addition to this study, I exceedingly recommend a copy of the Original Text in Hebrew, that has been translated into English and is a credible source for future research.

I am convinced that the making of Adam and Eve was unauthorized and that Almighty God did not give the confirmation to the <u>Lord God</u> to replicate that which He had already created.

Whenever one operates out of authority things tend to fall apart, "please understand that having an ability to make does not always mean permission to create." God is sovereign, and a merciful God, who sent Christ Jesus among Humanity to fix the brokenness and possibly restore mankind and womankind back to their original purpose and that is to live life abundantly.

However, abundance is enjoyed best when one's steps ordered by God. Everyone, please find what's your life line and live in abundance. Christ Jesus is a pure light in the darkness, and through Christ Jesus direction can be found, even in this 21st century. So many people are hurting and need answers, God, please help us.

Request

God in the name of Christ Jesus, I pray that my Book is a life changing blessing and bring light to dark spiritual places. While providing clarity on biblical teachings, interests, concerns, and questions that are not always easily found or discussed at a church or among believers in Christ Jesus. I pray after this study of literature all readers will stand more firm and denounce Satan's evil agendas that keep people trapped in the Garden of Eden Mindset, Amen.

Keep Pressing

Now, before diving directly into my extensive research and the revelations God revealed to me during a time of painful frustrations, as I sought out answers for a better life condition.

―

Let me start off with some snapshots of my childhood experiences, to give an idea of where my faith in God through Christ Jesus started. My mission is to provide a practical understanding while abstracting a relatable approach reflecting a series of events on my life's journey.

WALK WITH ME THERE IS MORE TO COME

Innocent

CHAPTER 1
INNOCENT

Before ever getting a formal Education or collecting scientific data to describe a quantitative meta-analysis for a descriptive research design. As a teenager, one who often read the Holy Bible sometimes came across writings that were un-applicable to a modern generation and consciously those particular scriptures became questionable. Of course, I did not dwell on my assumptions and took each word at face value. Because after all, it is the Holy Bible, right? Wrong.

In all things get an understanding and research other credible sources. Being one of Biblical Faith, I once too did not want to hear what anyone else had to say about God, Jesus or the Holy Bible, and primarily if it was rhetoric not of my faith because I was content and confident in what I believed. Although today I am still satisfied and assured, it is because I focused in on what God was trying to show me, while providing exposure to sound knowledge for victory over my life and being able to recognize distractions.

Often, only a few will seek additional research pertaining the Holy Bible, and unfortunately, many unwise teachers will teach the Holy Bible as the only credible source. Many are unwilling to see the whole picture that the Holy Bible is a summary of Events, Histories, Testaments, Prophecies, and Life Instructions. More importantly, understanding that some scriptures have been tampered with and revised by evil or misguided humans of the past and present.

Example of tampering with the Holy Bible: See Ephesians 6:5-9 (KJV) that states, "Obey your earthly Masters," that scripture is interference to victory and freedom. How? Because God once departed the red sea, to end slavery, for the people of Egypt. In addition, God allowed His son Christ Jesus to die, so Humanity may be spiritually free from all bondage. Therefore Ephesians 6:5-9, contradicts the character of the most-high God, by comparison, and His historical biblical behavior.

Unfortunately, many People go around putting standards on People as a form of control stating self-made principals as requirements for one to get to heaven or be considered a Christian, but the reality most of their input has no validity of being a sin nor is it God's Authentic Word. Study to know for thou self, Please, and know that Empowered People do not have to submit to corrupt Authority. God has given power within to destroy the yoke of bondage on any level of one's life.

Researchers, Leaders, and Church Assemblers purchase a copy of the Original Text because it has been translated and not interpreted, all in which there is a difference between the two termed words. After the study, demonstrate a comparative textual analysis by examining both texts, to see the changes made, along with the manipulation used, opposed to the Original Hebrew Text.

History Tip:

The King James Version of the Holy Bible is documented to be revised eight different times and could be more times, what research show, is that eight times were revised while he was alive. It is essential to know the history of King James before getting back up there aggressively preaching one's head off with weak facts and lightweight substance. In this study, while growing, along with extensive research and simply just walking with God through Christ Jesus as I'm being shown the way, to bring forth understanding.

I made sure that my usage of literature I referenced using the King James Version was a match or 99.9% match to the translation of the Original Hebrew Text, word for word and understanding for understanding before adding in my book.

Note that King James gathered scholars and holy people that were also scholars to translate the original text given to him. Subsequently, some things were changed, if one were to obtain the Original Hebrew text and compare the King James' Version, then the data described would confirm any doubt or misunderstanding. People, it's okay to go beyond the Holy Bible to gather factual research, because it not only improves one's message but also helps People more efficiently, because after all, is that not the purpose?

Live Your Best Life!

Yes, there are spiritual and physical systems designed to keep humanity trapped in an ongoing cycle rather it's dealing with depression, living in poverty, struggling to fit in, wrestling with bodyweight, body image, or never feeling quite whole. These lists of distractions can go on and on, but here's a reminder, never to forget, that God Almighty has given us the authority to stand against these vices and take our Life back fully.

The enemy first tries to attack the mind, and before one knows it, the war and frustration have already started in one's mind, and if not careful Satan and the Devil will team up leaving you feeling some type of way. All while pulling down the self-esteem and weaken the physical health condition to the point of not recognizing self anymore, "But God." Please stand in the Authority that was once delivered by God to live in fullness. Keeping the integrity of GOD's word clean and pure, so whenever someone seeks for answers or search for change, clear direction is available, in the hope of restoration. A path that will ensure those individuals will part take in an uncontaminated ministry in an effort toward wholeness.

After going through the vicissitudes of life and observing the correlation of the laws and standards listed in the Holy Bible. Several scriptures were not reflecting the Almighty God that I had come to know and it troubled me greatly. As I continued to study, more red flags were raised, and I came to a point to pursue precise findings from credible sources to bring remedy to that in which was sought.

※

Please note, my God experience was not a forced belief nor was my experience influenced by brainwash methods used to the view Christianity as the only way to know God. In my life, there have been some challenging circumstances and hopeless situations, and when I called out to God for help, He came to my rescue.

Many occurrences I have experienced are without question that it was God who moved on my behalf. God is real to me because He made Himself known as a reliable source that changed everything.

So I don't try to adjust anyone to believe God is true, because at the end of the day, every person is still responsible for how he or she functions themselves toward humanity.

Let's used the word Christian or Christianity to describe someone's faith. For starters, it's important to know they are just words and that alone ought not to be an issue. The overall concern should be how one conducts his or her selves representing and respecting God's Creation. Walking daily with God through Christ Jesus while building a relationship in prayer, will help a person filter or take inventory how he or she conducts their life.

Meaning genuine communication with God, one becomes more mindful of their behavior and is less willing to say or do any and everything without filters (heart conviction and consciousness). God's Spirit comes with so many benefits that meet the needs of the human spirit. God's spirit encourages one's soul to live better and operates in being the best possible upstanding person at all times, even when no one is around.

Until that concept is fully understood many will forever not figure out why there is such a great passion for the belief of Christianity all across the World. And let's be real here for a second, some people just want to do whatever, say whatever, however, to whomever, whenever, without any form of spiritual checks and balances. Usually, that kind of person get upset when they encounter other people who choose a different path that conflicts or contradicts their way of life.

Certainly, God will not force Himself on anyone that does not want His presence. These naysayers often say Christianity is fake, but the ones who speak this kind of rhetoric are never really searching for any truths. Why? Because they enjoy being unfiltered and will try to shut down anyone or anything that offers recommends or suggestions otherwise.

So whenever encountering folks who conduct themselves like that, just keep it moving, because they never really want to know God in a real way nor at least try to get an understanding.

They are very quick to augured why things are not right, followed by the Holy Bible is made up. Well, I will agree that some things in the holy bible have been added and changed by deceptive humans.

Designed to complement their hidden corrupt agendas while quoting misleading biblical scriptures to validate their ideas and beliefs on how they think a person should live according to their rules. Of course, those parts of the holy bible do become "human-made doctrine" and not God appointed. Especially the laws and standards in some scriptures that would never apply to this generation, yet many will say that it is God's will. But one who has an actual relationship with God can discern the real truth of God's character.

That way, even in those lies, misconceptions, and false doctrines within the Holy Bible, God will still reveal His presence to anyone who desires. Many beautiful things in the Holy Bible are true and does benefit the whole livelihood of humanity.

What I settled from observation, is that just because an individual whom has not experienced God, does not give anyone the right to denounce someone else's experience with knowing God.

One thing is for sure God is real, and He will continue to be so, even when it is not acknowledged or recognized. When seeking God in truth and sincerity through Christ Jesus, wisdom and understanding become more accessible regardless of how many parts of the Holy Bible have been tampered or twisted for corrupt agendas. God is love, and He will meet anyone right where they are.

<Fast Forward>

As a young boy, often I would get these robust stomach pains, followed by sickness and vomiting. During those occurrences, I was not a Christian, but I knew enough to call upon the name of Jesus for help and healing. Many occasions my skin would randomly break out into what is known as heat bumps, and it did not matter if I was playing outside or swiftly moving. Perhaps the bumps were due to over excitement or some type allergic reaction.

Nevertheless, suddenly the bumps would break out all over my arms, and neck. Whereas once my body temperature cooled down the heat bumps slowly faded away. The reaction was so frustrating each incidence especially to a kid who was trying to play.

After overcoming those health issues, a few years later my lower back would go out. For instance, a single arm reach would quickly pull or stain parts of my back muscles. Often drenched in tears due to the pain, because any kind body movement would only worsen the pain. For the life of me could not understand why I was experiencing so many difficulties.

So I began to pray for healing against whatever was going wrong with my body, and through it all Jesus healed my body.

I was not raised up in a religious household, and my immediate family was often dysfunctional. However, no matter how our opinions varied, at the end of the day, we all stood together as one unit.

Although our household was not what one called a devout Christian's home, that more so embraced the diversity of all kinds of music, lifestyle choices, food, art, other religious briefs, and cultures.

Helen Wilbert-Jenkins, Grandmother, in fact, believed in the existence of GOD and Christ Jesus. Early on Helen participated greatly in the activities held at her hometown's church. Though, one night after a church service Helen came home with a look of deep thought on her face and slowly took off her jewelry, her shoes, and her makeup. Then she walked out into the cool country's night air of our front porch and sat there for about an hour.

Inside looking out, I became scared that a wild animal might attack my grandmother and so I went onto the front porch and stood right beside her.

Helen, I asked, (during those times Helen did not want any of us to call her "grandmother") are you okay? Helen replied yes, I said, please come inside, it is dark outside. She said, oh nothing going to get me out here; I will come inside after a while.

❧

However, I did not accept her response, because my Grandmother was my heart and I wanted to protect her, even if it meant me being afraid of the dark. As Helen sat there in deep thought, I waited right next to her as we listened to the crickets creaked and frightening sound of the wild in the woods. I leaned over on her shoulder and asked what's wrong? Helen replied, "I am not going to church anymore," and so she never did for whatever reason(s).

Every month like clockwork, Helen would send her church dues by one of the local deacons who attended regularly. From time to time she would remind that Deacon she wanted to be buried right next to her mother's grave. (Helen's wishes was carried out).

❧

Before Helen's death, she kept this huge white Holy Bible on top of a cabinet or shifter-row as she called it. In front of that Bible is a picture which depicts the scene of Jesus at the last supper in a 3D format. A beautiful Holy Bible with quality pictures in color that demonstrate varies scenes illustrating a particular biblical scripture for that chapter.

This Bible was special to Helen because this is where she stored all kind of important papers, phone numbers, and family pictures right between its pages. I'm not sure what caused her to stop attending her church, but some nights I would find her reading the scriptures in that large white Bible and the look on her face was of peace which gave me peace.

Even though she stop going to her church, Helen held church gatherings at her home. Occasionally my Grandmother would have prayer meetings and Bible study in her living room. Some of the women in the nearby communities came and would sing, pray and cry. They sought after hope and strength for their everyday walk of life.

Each time everyone gathered someone would break out into song with "this little light of mines I'm going to let it shine." Over time the prayer meetings ceased, and we did not come together for Bible study anymore.

Faith Becoming Real for Real

CHAPTER 2
FAITH BECOMING REAL FOR REAL

Growing up, I had many struggles, as I tried to fit in or be accepted by the in-crowd all through elementary, junior high and early high school. However not accepted, but instead bullied at school almost every single day up until the 10th grade. I remember one day in the 9th-grade science class, everyone in the class was sectioned off in their clicks laughing and talking while waiting for class to start.

Whereas each time I tried to engage in conversation, some of my classmates would be so mean spirited toward me, and at that moment I remember feeling lesser, and my conversation was not valued. The following year arrived, which was my 10th-grade year of high school. I decided to create this hard persona of a tuff guy who was not going to take any guff from nobody, and that if anyone said or looked at me the wrong way, we were going to fight.

Now of course what was wrong with that idea, it was not my character, and most of all my Grandmother had not raised me to conduct myself in such a manner. Not liking the person, I was becoming, yet no matter how nice toward some of my peers at school, it did not matter they still were bullies.

Of course, I was not afraid of any of them, and indeed, I could very well defend myself. I decided to be cordial with everyone, even when some was not cordial.

Mrs. Levon Goins, Louisiana, an English Teacher, and a Christian who taught at my high school. Houses so many excellent qualities, and is a very positive forward-thinking person. Mrs. Goins always greeted me with a smile and carried a very sweet, yet strong demeanor about herself.

In knowing her, what became so dear to my heart even until this present day, is that Mrs. Goins treated me like a person and listened to what I had to say. Mrs. Goins valued my input inside her classroom and did not allow any of her students to talk negatively toward me or to each other.

One semester with the school principal's approval, Mrs. Levon Goins launched a high school level course called I CAN. An experience that empowered and encouraged her students to become the very best he or she set out to be.

The educational course I CAN was a very fun class, and I got to witness a professional laid back down to earth side of Mrs. Goins. She embraced the class with her wisdom and recognized our transitioning from teens into young adults. Mrs. Goins is a light, and she spoke life to her students.

I observed how firm Mrs. Goins stood against adversity and in her standing I never saw her Christian behavior change. Her example strengthened and encouraged me to continue conducting myself in good manners.

Shortly afterward I denounced putting on the tuff guy

demeanor because I did not want to be recognized as a bad behaving student nor damage the status of having an excellent school record that might impede me from future financial inclined opportunities. Readers character is everything.

Mrs. Levon Goins if you are reading this, please know I walked away from all of your classes feeling greater about myself. Mrs. Goins what an honor it is to know you and to have shared in your gifts of knowledge and divine wisdom. Please know I volleyed higher and reached destinations that only happen because of "light." Thank You, and I Love You So Much! God Bless.

Forever Grateful
Thank You!
Mrs. Levon Goins

During my early high school phase, I already had joined Mt. Pleasant Baptist Church and was a member there for about three or four years. I acceded to the adult gospel choir and in my mind being the good Christian, but the reality I was still lost and did not understand the fullness of Christ Jesus.

Going to church was something to do, and it felt good being in a positive environment, to say the least. Even though involved in church activities and events, I still did not quite fit in and was internally oppressed from the verbal abuse brought on by many other outside sources non-church related.

These individuals spoke deadly words into my life, and it spiritually left me broken and carrying around unwanted low self-esteem. Too ashamed to share my feelings with anyone it was hurting me, nor did anyone ever pulled me aside to help me understand.

Because of their treatment and having no one to confirm otherwise. I began to believe the mean-spirited things that were said and girls seemed to be the only group of people that would play with me without being bullied or called names.

So I started having mannerism like the girls because their behavior was much more positive. I fully trusted them and was comfortable with them just being myself, but once the name calling started, I felt betrayed because genuinely I saw them as my friends.

No one has a right to bully, pick on, discriminate, beat up, injury or murder anyone because they like something different, live differently, or just trying to find their way. Acting in violence toward these individuals is not God. Let us all remember in order to work together all things must be done in decency and in legal order and that applies to all parties involved.

Pinky, a friend, mentor, and a Sunday school teacher at Mt

Pleasant during that time would invite me to travel as she visited other local churches events, such as musicals, revivals, retreats, etc. Pinky became my hero, often she would invite me over for dinner after church, and her son would give me free haircuts, thanks.

Pinky always encouraged me that I am somebody and because of that I am forever grateful for her, and the kindness shown. While those moments were fantastic, still within lied brokenness bound by low self-esteem.

Pinky
I am honored to know You
Thank You So Much!

One day a miracle happened, a lady by the name of Vivian Thomas-Ellis, who came to Mt Pleasant after being hired on as one of the new musicians. Many of us in the choir had never seen anyone play the organ the way she can nor had heard anyone sing like this Woman of God can.

Vivian, anointed and holy ghost filled, and the power in her singing many times would cause some of us to forget to sing our next part of that song. We were so mesmerized by her gifts because Vivian sang like Jesus had taken a seat right in front of her organ.

Vivian growled like a "Mighty Lion" and I believe is called to sing to the Nations. She is one who lives a lifestyle backing up her song.

Of course, often whenever there is change, or something new there go those bitter know it all church folks hating with their personal beliefs and resistance on how the church is traditionally done. These kinds of limited thinking and lost individuals cannot see the miracle sent by God until they have aborted their blessing and that person leaves.

※

Meanwhile, I developed a friendship with Vivian, and she would pick me up on her way to choir rehearsal. Not only was Vivian a musician at our church, but she was also the head music player at her home church and a District Choir President for the Church of God in Christ, Greater Ouachita District in Monroe Louisiana.

One night she invited me to their revival at her home church, and I experienced a church service like no other before. God's presence grabbed hold to my hurt and began to repair my broken spirit.

Weeks after the revival was well over and things just did not go back to as usual, and I wanted to know more about Jesus in a for real way.

I asked a neighbor up the street to take me down to her church for Sunday school over at Dubach Church of God in Christ, in Dubach Louisiana. He said, are you sure you want to go down there with "them people." I said, yes please take me, and I will find a way back somehow.

Vivian was so kind to me, I lived about 13 minutes out of the way from the church, but every Sunday, Vivian would come pick me up. Earlier on sometimes after church service, I would overhear some of the church members tell Vivian something like "that's too far" or "you don't mind driving way up there" etc. Whereas, I would hear Vivian say, "oh it's not far at all, it just 9miles". To me, it sounded like those individuals were trying to convince Vivian to no longer pick me up.

Nevertheless, I will never forget Vivian's honesty, her willingness to help me, kindness, generosity, good food, and most of all how she did not count me out. Vivian helped me until her car broke down, and during that rough patch, her Dad, Pastor Lenard Thomas filled in the gap, along with my lovely dear friends Mr. David Fields and Mrs. Virginia Dunn-Fields.

I would spend the whole day with her and her family in wait for the Sunday's evening service Young People Willing Worker (YPWW). Later I joined the District Choir in Monroe, and Vivian would get off work in another city, drive all the way back to pick me up for choir rehearsal. Once rehearsal finished, she would drive me all the way back home, and sometimes rehearsal ended late; and then there was the driving to the District meetings itself. Vivian had a full schedule, and when I look back at all those moments, it was indeed nothing but the empowerment of the Holy Ghost, the favor of God, and the heart of an excellent person.

Pastor Thomas and her mom, First Lady Thomas, treated me like a son and welcomed me in their home where I sometimes stayed nights over and ate delicious meals. Good gracious Missionary Thomas could cook, and I thought now nobody could cook like my grandmother Helen, for she was cold in her kitchen. I told my Grandmother one day, I said, Nana, Vivian's mom is cold in the kitchen too, she laughed.

To make a very long story short, after I heard the word of God in a very different way I began to seek Jesus Christ even the more. Because there at that church, I saw there was different kind of life, righteous living. Holy people that praised God and spoke life to dead spiritual places, all while rebuking the evil works of Satan and they taught in LOVE.

I needed a new start, and of course, I left Mt Pleasant Baptist Church and became a member there at Dubach COGIC.

It was truly a church house of delivering power, and by hearing the sound word of God, my self-esteem increased, and I finally started loving me but was still a work in progress.

Please note I am not stating that one church is better than the other. I moved churches because I experienced God in a very real way and that is the key no matter where one worships make sure by all means God is in the midst and that your soul is spiritually fed and that you as a member can implement that experience into your everyday life.

The late Pastor, Elder Lenard Thomas, and the late First Lady, Missionary Mandy Caldwell-Thomas of Dubach COGIC decided to have an old fashion 3-day tent revival outside of the church. OMG, that Church service at the tent revival was amazing to the point my heart was spiritually convicted in God's presence.

I asked Christ Jesus for forgiveness for not always being the best possible person, and I tarried before Him to change, and Jesus did change my heart.

I sought after Christ Jesus because I desired restoration and healing from all the years of bondage, pain and verbal abuse. Weeks went by, and I kept on reading the Bible and continued to tarry, fast, and pray.

One day while I sat home, I overheard someone said, a revival was going on in Arcadia, Louisiana. Came to find out the revival was at one of my neighbors' church, who lived across the way. In the country across the way does not necessarily mean a next-door neighbor, but nearby in that area.

Calvin Wortham, a prior neighbor, the Pastor there, whom I knew. Wortham was friendly and invited to his church some Sundays. Wortham and his wife, Brenda, both drove over and picked me up for assembly at their church. Even though, their church was in the opposite direction of where I lived in that area. Nevertheless, the Wortham's Family went about six minutes out of their direction to pick me up.

Meanwhile, during those times, I did enjoy service when I visited because I was seeking something different than the Mt. Pleasant experience. At the first stages of fellowship with the Wortham's, I was just trying to find my way, mimicking a form of church experience, but not quite understanding God's presence and missing the opportunity of how to go forth or operate thereof in, which then left my praise operating in an offset praise.

However, near the end of my season of fellowship with the Wortham's, by this time, I had become a part of Dubach Christ of God in Christ Church, and so my offset praise had turned into being on one accord praise (Glory!) which brought forth real worship because of victory that was upon my life.

Honestly, I don't know how Mr. Wortham and I paths crossed? I'm not sure why they took the liberty to embrace me with kindness? Whereas, I'm grateful they did, Thanks, and God Bless!

<Fast Forward>

When we got to the church, there was a guest Preacher that he had invited and as this man of God began to preach a word from God that spoke to all my hurts, problems, concerns, struggles and it touched the very core of my inner man which is the soul.

God's power pulled me closer to His presence, and as I began to praise Christ Jesus and lifted up my hands in total surrender, the next words came out my mouth was, "YES LORD" unto Christ Jesus.

It was utter that came from the core depths of my soul, my heart, my mind, and my whole will said YES, and at that moment I received more new life through and through. Jesus opened my eyes and unlocked the limitations that had me bound.

I understood love, I felt love, and most of all loved myself, and later I received the Comforter. I saw who I am and the way that God saw me and so began my journey in Christ Jesus. A journey leading me back to the state God wants every Human, and that's walking in His presence of light, and wholeness of Life.

I was at the age of 15 years old when I came to know Christ Jesus and the Almighty God in a very real way. Since the awakening, have I made mistakes or sin? Yes, I have, I am even willing to confess some pleasures I enjoyed and even loved. However, over the years I went through many struggles and hardships in my life, I slowly pulled away from the church and the faith.

I started listening to the wrong kind of People and including my very own self-desires, and it got me into a lot of trouble. I placed myself in harm's way, but God, you feel me. I felt awful afterward and sometimes could feel God's anointing leaving my body.

So I know and understand life's ups and downs, and I know what it's like to mess up. However, right now I am still standing on the promises of God through grace and mercy.

What is most important to me is being honest and transparent about who I am, so that I may always be free, even if that means exposing my weaknesses and struggles. Someone could be struggling with very same issues, and my testament may help someone get through. So please don't stop being encouraging and share the goodness of Jesus. We have overcome by the words of our testimony.

Don't stop because there will always be someone who hides secrets and always defensive, but speculates or is suspicious about everybody else, while never forthcoming about themselves. These individuals never have any real facts and rely on little to no valid evidence. Then under the same breath will try to instruct another person how he or she should live. Next Please.

Remember there will always be nosey judgmental folks lurking around with no real genuine concern about one's well-being because their only demonic mission is to see have you failed yet. Be mindful of trolls for they will always come around trying to use what they know, or think they know about one's personal business all while trying to use that information as a weapon later.

Vivian Thomas-Ellis
Thank You For Everything
I Never Shall Forget
Your Kindness

Homeless

CHAPTER 3
HOMELESS

"Sincere tears holds a story that only God and Christ Jesus understands."

~Nitoric Jenkins~

During my second year of undergraduate study, I lost my part time job, and could no longer pay the rent, and shortly afterward I lost my apartment. I end up staying with a couple of awful people but moved out very quickly having no place safe to live with the small amount of money. I became homeless and so by word of mouth I heard about a place called the Young Men Christian Association (YMCA) a homeless shelter.

At the YMCA one could rent a room with a shared bathroom by paying a weekly or monthly fee at a low cost. So I went by the YMCA casa boom location and took a tour of the facility. Let's just say I did not want to live there, and at that moment I felt like a complete loser. The YMCA was not only a gym for people to workout at, but some locations offered a private side for homeless people.

I moved into the YMCA because there was nowhere else to go that would understand my vision or the plan for my life and

so I needed space for it to manifest, and going back home was not an option. So I fought and endured for my vision to manifest. By this time, I got hired on at the Banana Republic store, Galleria Houston and purchased a used car (eventually, that got repossessed too). I fell into depression, and I was on my way out of "here."

Before the depression, I did not think much of it, because to me depression was something that may have been made up or an over aggravation. Depression grabbed a hold to me, and it felt like I would never be whole again. During the late nights all alone was the worst times for me and it got so bad each morning when I opened my eyes I asked why did I wake up? Only to relive it all over again, I wanted to die.

※

My routine was, I would get up and put on my what I thought was my happy face. The pain was so great I eventually went to the Doctor, and he knew what was going right away and offered me a prescription to take. I got highly offended, and I said, I am not crazy. The Doctor laughed and said, I did not mention that, and he explained to me that the pills would only relax me and give me some relief.

I went ahead took the prescription, but I did not want a "happy pill." A week went by, and I still refused to take the pills, but the stress aching pain was getting worse and I struggled until finally breaking down and taking one.

Low and behold I felt some relief in my face, but my faith in God would not allow me to believe that I was going to live life being on what I called a happy pill. Please understand I could feel death licking the very essence of my life, and I was dying.

Each day I would put on the happy face, but one day a

Professor by the name of Dr. Esther Thomas looked out into her classroom and called me up to her desk.

Dr. Thomas asked me my name, I responded, then she asked, what is wrong with you? I said, nothing is wrong with me, but she rebutted with, I see something, and in your time you will tell me.

Next time in class, Dr. Thomas looked over at me and said come here, something is wrong, and I responded, I am alright, and nothing is wrong with me offensively. The next class Dr. Thomas, looked over at me and said come here, let's go outside and talked. Dr. Thomas said, I am not trying to be nosey, but something keeps telling me to talk to you, even though you say nothing is wrong but something is, and she asked, what is troubling you, Nitoric?

I said, Dr. Thomas, I am homeless and lost everything, and live in a homeless shelter. Dr. Thomas said, talk to Dr. John Williams, and inform him of our discussion; I believe he can help you. Dr. Thomas told me how to find his office in the building, but I did not want to go and expose myself any further. What I have learned in this life, is that some wounds need to be exposed in order to heal.

Thank You
Dr. Ester Thomas
Thanks for Believing in
Your Students

Meanwhile, I went and found his office, I walked in, greeted by his secretary. I asked was Dr. John Williams available and she said sure, he is in his office walk over knock on the door. I introduce myself to Dr. Williams, he was very kind and welcomed me in his office. I told him Dr. Ester Thomas sent me and the reason why.

Dr. Williams "heard" me and then he started speaking life back to me right there on the spot. Dr. Williams said, "Nitoric you do not remind me of a person who is not trying to be somebody, and I can tell you are a decent, respectable young man. Nitoric, you will not fail due to unfortunately things that have to happen in your life, but you will win."

Phew! Excuse me for a sec, (Glory!!!).

Dr. John Williams
I am Forever Grateful
I Never Shall Forget
Your Kindness Sir

I had not experienced such genuineness in such a long time. I had started to believe kind people did not exist anymore but the love Dr. Ester Thomas and Dr. John William showed toward me gave me hope, and it did not stop there.

Dr. Williams, the Assistant Dean, could have quickly sent me out of his office and treated me like a number, after all, it was not his problem. Instead, Dr. Williams reached out and helped me and made it clear as the day that if I ever needed help again let him know. Dr. Williams walked with me every step of the way until I reached graduation. He even went to meetings regarding me graduating on time and sometimes arrived before I did.

I was a transfer student, and he values students, Dr. Williams made sure all I's dotted and all T's crossed. Dr. John Williams, I never shall forget you and all that you did for me. Dr. Williams, you blew life back into me, Thank You.

Meanwhile, I still wrestled with depression, and it seemed like there was no way out from the spiritual shackles that held me bound. I went to the Pastor at the church I was attending in Houston, Texas. It was at the Sunday's night service; I made up my mind that I was not going to take any more pills and that I was going to sit that bottle of pills on the altar and leave them there.

But I forgot them back at the shelter, and I didn't realize it until when I got near the altar, I noticed another church member had placed their pill bottle on the altar, LOL. The Pastor was near the middle of the aisle, and I turned to the Pastor and informed him that I felt very sick and that I felt like was about to die. Immediately I looked up toward heaven and said, God if you don't help me I am going to die.

I was so tired of fighting but that Pastor looked into my eyes and said, with authority brother you are going to live and not die. Readers, God can work a miracle so fast sometimes it takes the senses to catch up or react to the miracle that just happened.

Now, remember, I was at church that Sunday's night service and Monday afternoon has arrived. Around noon was the time I usually went to get lunch and then drive back to the campus, where I sat and ate lunch in my car inside the university's car garage.

I sat in my car of the car garage because it was kind of like a safe zone to gather my thoughts right before the next class started. While I sat there, I noticed I felt magnificent, oh but wait until the night I thought to myself.

Monday night, I slept all night long, but it still did not register with me what had happened. Tuesday arrived and at noon, as usual, I sat in my car eating, and I said to self, hmm I feel excellent, but then I thought to myself wait until tonight. Wednesday came noon I was sitting in my car eating, and I thought again to myself, wow I slept all night and mmm I feel Good! And then it hit me; I realized God had healed me, and it took three days to grasp what happen.

⁕

Being it was Wednesday a Bible study night at the church, (which was like going to a regular Sunday morning church service) I could not drive my car to church any faster. I use to think it was strange when I see someone run around inside the church house.

But that night I asked the Pastor on a note through one of the Deacons if I could give my testimony, and the Pastor responded yes. As I began to tell of the goodness of God through Christ Jesus before I knew it, I took flight. God put running in feet to let me know that I was free and that the chains of depression no longer had me bound. God cast down that spirit of depression and took it away from me. To GOD be the Glory!

Shortly afterward, I found out about the YMCA downtown Houston that had a similar shelter set up, (however, since then that old building has been torn down) and so I moved there. The YMCA downtown is where I met Ms. Damitra Myles, Resident Program Director. A few months went by, and Ms. Myles called me into her office and said, "Nitoric I do not know what it is about you, but there's something about you, and I want to help you."

Ms. Myles said I work with a program that is a part of the United Way and they give monies to our program to help pay some of the resident's shelter fees, and I am going to add you to the list.

Ms. Myles looked at me and said, Nitoric don't give up. I lived there for about two years as I build myself up and move into an apartment.

You see, the "hurt," of going through did not quite let me see then, but when I look back at all the ways God made for me. Phew! Excuse me for a second! Glory!

Thank You
Ms. Damitra Myles
For Helping Me
Love You Dear
What a Wonderful Person
You Are

Trying to Make Sense of Things of GOD

Chapter 4
Trying to Make Sense of Things of GOD

"It is not in God's Divine Will, for Humanity to work all their life just to pay off a house and finally, drive an expensive automobile".

~Nitoric Jenkins~

A few months into the year of 2016, I needed some answers as to why my life expectations and heart desires were not adding up with my faith. I started questioning God and things in the Holy Bible because it did not match His character that I had come to know.

I asked God what's going on because my faith aggressively was shaken to the very core of unbelief and it felt like everything good in me was being slowly ripped out. I thought about all those things I invested my time into and how I poured all my trust in God. I began to greatly wonder why God ever contested with a fallen angel that He made, regarding the redemption of Humans. I was hurting from life's blows, and it was getting harder to "believe in" or have confidence in God. Seeing how Satan operates in power and the influence of using people to accomplished evil deeds.

I was completely and utterly frustrated by not being able to see God's People have more businesses, apartment properties, homes, job opportunities, and more. I asked God, why so many Christians or Faith believers do not have anything worth anything that maximizes the everyday experiences bringing profits to their livelihood.

I said God, please look at my environment because everyone else around here is building but Christians. They do not have businesses that I recognize, and I wondered how could we say we are in Christ Jesus who once was a carpenter who built things, yet we don't build anymore.

I told God, the only thing I see are bigger churches built and that is it. Accustomed to Black churches, I cried, God look at the Black Churches and the thousands and thousands of believers gathering at these churches, yet as a whole, we still have absolutely nothing worth much of nothing.

And the hand few who does have money, do not justify the total ratio of lack. I cried what is wrong with this picture because in Christ Jesus there is the fullness of life, light, and a sound mind to work and move toward a better life both spiritually and physically. Where is our help I asked?

I reminded God of how I had gone to college twice, earned a Bachelors and then a Master's Degree and now working on my Doctrine. I screamed why it is so hard to find regular work, a great job, and gainful employment. I got exhausted of seeing church people shouting and praising over the bread crumbs of life, and it felt shameful saying we are serving an Almighty God, but over half of believers are living in poverty and are financially broke.

❦

I grew tired of hearing testimonies of people praising God for getting a hold to some money to pay their light bill. I wanted to hear people of God shout and testify of they were a stakeholder at the light company or owned something that will benefit their lives entirely.

Why wasn't my faith not backing up His word I asked? For it is the very core of what I had come to believe that God can do exceedingly and abundantly above all that we ask or think, according to the power that works in us. I screamed from the top of my lungs, "where are you God in us?"!

People all across the world, I DO NOT believe it is in God's divine will or plan for us as people to work all our life just to pay off a house and a car. Never having new ideas to become prosperous, never building anything that would be a long-term increase in value through overall economic income gains for generations to come.

Too many Christians do not have shares or stocks or no long term profit sharing investments, and their children not having college funds, and one can forget about an inheritance left.

Many believers believe that the wealth of the wick is being stored up for them. Maybe so, but if you have never done anything with your financial enhancements, do you believe you can manage someone else's money effectively? The answer is no you cannot and no you will not and until the mindset changed many will forever be in poverty and the same bondage will be passed down until broken.

A consistent relationship with God through Christ Jesus is necessary because God is not a magic won, but a Strategic God and not a conversation piece to place on one's social resume because it sounds good to impress people. Please tap into a rim of God and discover the worth of life and living life. Struggling and going without is not God's will for our life. I cried out God, please help me, because I am so lost, and asked how can a fallen angel have caused and is causing all this pain among humanity?

With complete frustration, I needed answers, and so I decided to go back and read where creation all got started in the book Genesis. Concluding there has to be something wrong with what's taught because I could not find anybody that could offer any real valid answers of that in which I sought after.

A vast majority of earnest church folks simply do not read to learn God, but instead, read to preach their sermons or get their message across with the intent of possibly reaching someone's life and bringing them closer to God through Jesus Christ. However, by the time real studying occurs, the majority of Church members has had some spiritual experience, and many filled with the Holy Ghost or Holy Spirit.

Though many church folks then take those spiritually experiences and run with it, and for years failing to realize what God did supernaturally in their life, has not even scratched the surface of how much more He can do in natural. Often God sends preachers who will attempt to teach something different from the norm, but Heaven forbids if church folks do not agree with that "something different" many church folks automatically go into speaking in tongues rebuking the right help that could have taken them to the next level in God.

Take notice as to why so many of the Saints of God children and grandchildren act nothing like the faith of their parents who are fully committed to God. Many of their children leave home and are not thinking anything about being saved, and it is the furthest thing from their minds. The reality saved or kept to them means poverty and not victory.

A great majority of the saint's children that didn't move away from home, but stayed around are spiritually broken and counting down days because putting on the church face has gotten unbearable.

Then there are those church children who just cannot take putting up a front anymore, and they completely change their whole outwardly appearance in the way they dress, style their hair, wear their clothes, the types of friends they hang with, etc.

Many are so unrecognizable as to ever come from among anybody's church. Please know I will not be shocked if some church folks disagree with me or even get very upset with my statements. Clutch a hold in advance, I do not care, and save the hate mail for it will not be entertained.

Too many people are hurting at these churches, and Sunday after Sunday and year after year very little has increased their livelihoods outside the four walls.

Meanwhile, the illusion of being blessed is bigger than ever before (just visit some of the surrounding churches). The common patterns are gigantic hats, expensive shoes, high-end suits, name brand handbags, nice cars, but most are financially balance at zero.

Many will have the nerve to shout and dance all over the church, over the fact they look like money, all while trying to persuade the congregation that this way of thinking is okay. So lost, let me know when the fairy tale is over, I got work to do.

To my celebrated black brothers and sisters. God has blessed several black men and black women in this generation to the point many are now millionaires. I am yet to see adequate resources "invested" back that represent black communities or developing black communities that create more business opportunities and better affordable housing. Giving a donation is not the solution unless the allocation of those funds are regularly tracked and monitored. Then the Donor seeks to witness the improvements made by that donation and not just the effort to get a tax write off.

Mimicking the Fallen

Over the years there have been a whole lot of arguing, fussing and the usage of obscene language against each other on national TV and nowadays it's called "shade." Those individuals participating, just so you know, that behavior further degrades the representation of black people.

One would have to be an entirely self-absorbed individual not to see this. Please be mindful that irrational behavior projected in those high places still reflects the perception of black people in the low places, and in many cases affect how blacks are viewed in normal society rather admitted or not. Currently, there is not a balance or variety of positive representation, and the aftermath is too great at our expense. If we came together, there would be more significant resources and taking the low road would not be the only available option. Usually, the ones who act like a raging buffoon personally don't feel the effects or experience the damage left behind.

Why? Because when it is all said and done, those individuals go back to their exclusive neighborhoods and lifestyles. While many of us are left to clean up the self-character assassinated residue left behind, and this madness has to stop.

The foundation has gotten weak, and upon experiencing societal changes, they are temporary because the number of concerned Leaders are too few. The follow-ups referencing to the significant changes from the 60's is no longer enough to discuss. Wasted efforts to smooth things out because our generation is not standing up more for equality. Please note that two or three cities that protests here and there of diverse groups of people cannot do it all by themselves.

I know it is very frustrating to see whenever that one black person stands up and fight against injustice, and then someone from the media goes finds a sellout to rebuttal against their grievance. Do not let those kinds of ignorant limited thinking people stop you from speaking out. A Big Thanks to all those who speak up, and speak out, keep standing for you are not alone. Despite those despicable clowns who try to reduce the urgency of social justice outcry.

Too many are afraid, yet are quick to fight against each other. Afraid? Oh because you might lose your job? Afraid? Because you don't want anyone to know you are against unfair treatment, yet you want fair treatment. Afraid? Because you have a mortgage to pay? Afraid? Because you cannot let your high-end cars go back?

What happens when you look around, and there is no one with ethics to be found? Then unqualified people take power, and the unemployment risk becomes much greater, as well as the chance of losing all those "things" that are so dear. People we must do better because we should know better and we have access to better. Instead of trying to be so grand and caught up in self-absorption, why not help change the course of humanity forever.

If Black Lives Matters, then let's all be mindful we all matter, and we should help each other before things get to those extremes. Because if real problems are not addressed prior, most efforts afterward will not be viewed as sincere awareness or genuine concern.

God has not blessed this generation of people with these all these talents, gifts, education, and money only to sit back and brag about having it. Nor does God want us to sit on these blessings and not utilize them for the maximum outcome. If we don't help each other effectively and in a positive life changing manner, then history is just going keep repeating another 60 years. Be thankful and help your fellow human come up as well or simply just be glad they came up.

Hundreds of educated black men and women graduate colleges around the United States every single semester and some end up going to work at unwelcomed places and if it was not for affirmative action well you know. What you all don't trust your ethnicity? Someone trusted and hired you. My thoughts might make some upset, and as usual, someone goes and find another black person to tear down another black person for speaking out about realities many black people experience.

All while in the same breath those self-haters will say these things does not exist because, after all, look at them, they made it. Wow, what a sick twisted lost mindset of any individual who thinks that just because he or she has made it, then everything must be okay or equal.

Thank God for the elders who fought so that we might have a chance in the pursuit of happiness. So many has taken our heritage and spit on it. God sees, and He knows, and one day those deeds will be held accountable. The media has done an excellent job of always giving a platform to buffoons on National TV. No longer showing a positive and real projection of successful black people and if any shown, it is so brief one could miss it. If there is anyone who does not have a clue, I highly recommend you find a clue and start listening.

Lastly, to all Americans and all people across the world who help support and represent positive reinforcements regarding black lives in referencing fairness toward humanity, Thank You!

Please note I am not referring to the Black Lives Matter movement in general, but what I will say based on my observation, it is not the movement itself their problem. Whereas, it is the power and profoundness behind those three words.

The people who want limitations on **Black Life period** are troubled the most by the added black awareness movement because it calls more attention to their common unfair treatment and unfair practices toward black people.

The Black Lives Matter Movement is another spotlight that once again positions those individuals to face the evil hidden inside their heart and the injustices they produce daily toward the black people or any persons they have wronged.

Of course, darkness never wants the light to shine, and the truth of the matter is, alone those three words packs a mean punch. All hatred regardless of their social status or skin color, simply just do not know how to stop it. Why? Because of its straightforwardness.

For them, it's like trying to halt the sun from shining, but absolutely cannot and that is just too much to process for a true ethnocentric person.

> *"Racist and hatred influenced people overall problem with the Black Lives Matter Movement, is the word choice listed within "the Black Lives Matter phase." Why? Because these three words are so simple a child can understand that someone is being left out. How can anyone truthfully speak against this movement to their children, without in return teaching their kids hatred and racism? For this movement is a two-edged sword and that is why the resistance is so great because it houses personal accountability in its pure form."*
>
> ~Nitoric Jenkins~

TAKE YOUR LIFE & FAMILY BACK!
Let's Break Bread

CHAPTER 5
LET'S BREAK BREAD

"Never think an Enemy is going to reveal their True Form day one, if so, then think again."

~Nitoric Jenkins~

The book of Genesis has been reviewed by thousands of people over and over for many years. The story of "IN THE BEGINNING" has been preached in many parts of the world at many church congregations, and even depicted and captured on film and presented on big movie screens.

What I am about to present to my audience of readers comes at an entirely different angle and per-spectrum from what many have come to believe, including myself. Shall we put on our spiritual lenses? Proceed. My faith, hope, and desires were not getting fulfilled, and I was getting fatigued from waiting for a blessing to come. After finally receiving a blessing, I would be too spiritually weary to enjoy the benefits of that blessing fully.

Because on occasions, something about that blessing would be not quite what I had in mind, and it left me very unsatisfied because it did not fulfill my expectations. Often, when I received

the blessing, I was going through wrestling stages of my life. One-half of my life would be perfect and another half not perfect.

For example, blessed with the car, but could not find work or sustain work to keep the vehicle, and by the time work was found, I no longer had the vehicle. Going from being happy about my blessing, to struggling to try to make myself happy about having that blessing. After experiencing this degree of chaos, all kinds of thoughts, feelings, and questions pulled and tore at the very core of my faith. I could not understand why life was hard just to obtain the normal things in life!

Especially being one who was grateful unto Christ Jesus and one who trusted and praised God for His goodness. Whereas, year after year and struggle after struggle, I screamed from the hurt on the inside, because the Biblical scriptures did not appear to work.

The thoughts in my mind were if I hear one more preacher, quote one more scripture as to why I am not receiving the desires of my heart, I am going scream! While I tried to grasp why God only would not just bless, thinking how much more faith needed to get God's Favor, the aching pain of waiting and longing for more began to set in cracks of my brokenness. I would wake up many days hearing myself moaning from the aches desperately seeking aid but could not find it anywhere.

I started questioning, crying, and begging manifestation, where Art Thou?! I grew tired of hearing and seeing people of God always needing to be encouraged in this faith, and so observation crept in speculating if the Holy word was slavery versus freedom.

The expectations of who God is came into question and caused me to wonder had the Holy Bible's Literature been twisted by some skilled demon. A great level of concern brew and manifestation was urgently needed, I grew tired in faith giving excuse after excuse as to why as a whole Christians are financially broke and never seeing productive life-changing Kingdom building. I looked over at my Bachelor's and Master's Degree, grasping for air brought on by the tightness of stress. Bearing what I once called victory now looked like a worthless failure. Help me, somebody! I screamed, anybody because this is too much, I thought about all I had invested over the years. Examining the circumstance that I might have been tricked and given fairy dust of false hope.

No this cannot be true because after all, it was Christ Jesus who came in and delivered me out of the things that had bound. I cried where is my HARVEST?! I asked God why Satan has so much power and why are so many Christians financially broke? Is the Bible made up?

Have a skilled Demon twisted the word to keep certain people bound? I told GOD the Bible is starting to feel like slavery and not freedom anymore. I cried, what are we up against?

And God simply showed me this.

> In the beginning, GOD created the heavens and earth (Genesis 1:1 KJV).

GOD said to me, "I did not create a garden, but I created the heavens and earth." Then God walked me through the whole chapter one of Genesis in which show the process of creation.

<Fast forward>

> And GOD said, let us make man in our image, after our likeness, and let them have dominion over the fish and of the sea, and over the fowl of the air, and over the cattle and over <u>all</u> the earth (Genesis 1:26 KJV).

Now, pay close attention to the scriptures for what I am about to show everyone, especially those individuals who do not researcher anything, yet try to defend what many has poorly taught or scanned through while "studying."

Please Note

The Original Hebrew text referenced the word "<u>human</u>" and not the word "man." Chapter 1 is not a summary, but whole separate occurrences of the event and should not compare to the timeline listed in Genesis Chapter 2:4

> So God created human in his own image, in the image of God created he him; <u>male</u> and <u>female</u> created he <u>them</u> (Genesis1:27 KJV).

Let us look at the word "So" it is an indication that God went ahead and made humans without any assistance.

Look at how verse 27 becomes very precise with its description. God created humans in His own image meaning He did not have any participation in the design of the human structure at this point. Then God categorized the human into male and female.

> And God blessed them, and God said unto them, be fruitful and multiply, and replenish the earth, and

> subdue and have dominion over the fish of the sea and over the fowl of the air, and over every living thing that moves upon the earth (Genesis 1:28 KJV).
>
> And God behold I have given you every herb bearing seed, which is upon the face of all the earth, and every tree, in which is the fruit of a tree yielding seed; to you, it shall be for meat (Genesis 1:29 KJV).

While I was researching for understanding, God then said to me; I did not put anyone to sleep to make a woman. God said, "I did it correctly the first time, and that female was already in my blueprint."

God said, "Nor did it take me to realize that the male needed a help mate, <u>I created it correctly the first time,</u> and it was good." At this point, I told God I'm listening.

<Fast Forward>

> And GOD saw everything that He had made and behold it was very good. And the evening and the morning were the sixth day (Genesis 1:31 KJV).
>
> And God blessed the seventh day and sanctified it: because that in it He had rested from all his work which God created and made (Genesis 2:3 KJV).

Created: just means to invent.

PART 2
Stop Trying to Copy God:
It Never Ends Well

I began to talk to God about what I felt, and He not only gave me some answers and showed me what was right under my nose the whole time. While during this research I was blown away by what's revealed to me. Please note everyone is entitled to believe whatever he or she chooses, and what is true, no matter whatever one's wants to believe, a fact will always be just that, a fact.

The making of Adam and Eve was not authorized and was not approved by God to build more humans. The male and female had already been instructed to go and be fruitful and multiply. Trying to copy God, it never ends well for those who do.

The unauthorized making resulted in the fall of Adam and Eve, because Adam and Eve's un-confirmed creation formed in error, and it was only natural they eventually would start acting by error because error only produces errors.

Even though the Lord God had the ability to form a "human" everything must be done in the will of the Almighty God, notice in the Genesis chapter 1, there was a conversation that said, "let us." There is something special about being on one accord in God.

The word **Lord** simply means the ability to operate in power given by **authority**. In Genesis Chapter 1, God himself had a brief conversation with everyone who had the "ability" to make a human, and HE suggested to them "let us make human."

They did not fully capture God's vision as to why He wanted to make a human in their image, and so God went ahead and created male and female in His image, and everything God made was good.

The error came when a replica or facsimile of God's creation done without getting God's final approval. God makes no mistakes and remember in Genesis 1 and 31: And God saw everything that He made and, behold it was very good. At this point, I was locked and listening as He began to show me the errors that lead to humanity's fall. Watch closely because here is where so many people get lost and try to smooth all the scriptures into one event.

> And the Lord God formed man of the dust of the ground and breathed into his nostrils the breath of life, and man became a living soul. (8) And Lord God planted a garden eastward in Eden; and put the man whom he formed (Genesis 2:7,8 KJV).

Formed: just means set up or establish.

God said, if I made humans in my image, then why would I need to breathe life into their nostrils because life means one is already breathing. God said everything I created I spoke it into its present state. God then said, I created the heavens and earth, why would I then create only one male human only to place him in a garden of Eden when I had already instructed humans. (See Genesis 1:28).

To be fruitful, and multiply and replenish the earth and subdue it: have dominion over fish of the sea, and over the fowl of the air, and over every living thing that moves upon the earth.

Notice God is about <u>increasing</u> and not lacking, and whatever we need, God has made it so that it always comes with an increase.

God then said humans are not to be bound in a garden, **God then asked me, who does this reminds me of?** I responded Satan, for he likes to keep people bound and placed in the corner of limitations.

People of God, can anyone see that by being bounded in a garden hinders the will to have dominion over the sea and every living thing that move on upon the earth right? Right, being bound in the garden opens the doors and give the intent to a form of slavery or isolation. People of God it is right there in the text; intelligent people of GOD get your power back. Again God did not create a garden, but He created the heavens and a whole big earth.

"Some Evils are not obliviously recognized."

~Nitoric Jenkins~

Understanding the Character and Nature of God

The Lord God mimicked **GOD'S creation** and whenever anyone tries to emulate someone's original work that individual(s) run the risk of high error.

One must completely understand a person's vision and purpose in totality and even then the odds of comprehending it 100% is never because we cannot operate successfully trying to own something that is somebody's else invention.

God said Nitoric you have been walking with me over 20 years now, and I stayed with you even the times when you sinned and messed up. I still loved you and showed you my Glory through Christ Jesus. I replied, yes God you have been there with me.

God said, when Humans makes a mistake or sin, I offer forgiveness with mercy and grace. I even proved my love in offering redemption by sending Jesus to die for ALL HUMANS so that everyone may have a chance at redemption.

Does kicking a Human out of the garden for making an error represent my character and nature? God said, "I offer forgiveness with mercy and grace." God then said keep reading there is more for you to see.

Now the serpent was subtle than any beast of the field which the Lord God had made. And he said unto the woman, Ye hath God said, Ye, shall not eat of every of the garden (Genesis 3:1 KJV).

Notice how the text indicates the Lord God made the subtle serpent breast, but look closer at the words used when the serpent, speaks to Eve, "Ye hath God said," notice how Lord God is not used? But the serpent uses the words, God said, because the serpent is lying about which Authority has instructed because even the serpent know the difference between the two authorities.

Eve was tricked into what appeared to be following instructions of God, then true; she would not die because God was never part of Eden's madness, so no, she would not have died.

However, it is that the Lord God made Eve and had dominion over her, the instruction was not to eat from that particular tree, and she did eat which brought forth judgment on her. Later, in the text Eve cried out, the serpent beguiled her in eating from that forbidden tree.

<u>Error number 1:</u>

A talking Snake that held a full conversation.

<u>Error number 2:</u>

The breast more intelligent than the Humans?

<u>Error number 3:</u>

A tree that held knowledge of good and evil.

Error number 4:

The serpent human abilities made out the error, and so the serpent operated in error.

Error number 5:

Taking the rib from Adam does not make her a wife, that made her a Family Member. Some things have been going on since the beginning of time.

This conduct is Not of the behavior and nature of God. And God will not withhold anything good from His people, and certainly, He does not need a tree to hold His mysteries.

> And when the woman saw that the tree was good for food, and that is was pleasant to the eyes and a tree to be desired to make one wise, she took of the fruit thereof, and did eat, and gave also unto her husband with her, and he did eat (Genesis 3:6 KJV).

If God has given instructions to subdue the earth and the fullness thereof, does that not mean one is already wise enough to handle the task at hand. The Devil will have us walking around thinking we are not capable, dumb, and lost. The Devil will have us thinking we are NOT worth anything or have the ability to accomplish anything of value.

Please know God has already placed down on the inside of everyone what he or she needs along with the capacity and wisdom to fulfill it. Humans were already validated in GOD's creation and eating a fruit did not give Humans that ability.

Their eyes were already opened, but being in the Garden of Eden caused them to be blind, bounded, and limited.

And the eyes of them both were opened, and they knew that they were naked; and they sewed fig-leaves together, and made themselves aprons (Genesis 3:7 KJV).

Is this not like the Devil, to have a person outside NAKED, exposing himself or herself inappropriately? People of God, I declare, and decree lets go deeper because it is necessary to learn more.

God will not have His people to be ignorant, are we or have we solely Restricted God through people at church and based ourselves on how one dresses, think, live, teach and preach? Do we stop there and miss the rest God has for us? The same kind of people will turn right around and call their way is Holy living and creating their doctrine as a road map for eternal life in God. Please get to know God for self, and being real with God, guarantees God will be real in return. Casting all one's cares upon Him, through Christ Jesus, and this route helps filter, holy from unholy, and clean, from unclean, a natural process.

Creating a pathway to a heart's conviction and therefore living blamelessly becomes a way of life complementing your lifestyle. The reason so many church People get frustrated by things they cannot live up too, because the reality is if it's not in one to do, then it will not produce.

Please embrace this concept and be found not saying: Well God knows my heart, it doesn't take all that, nobody is perfect. With that kind of statements, what happens is that individual get nowhere in the Kingdom of God, and 30 years later still in the church drinking milk. Why? Because they think its meat ate, but no my friends, it is just hard lumps of old dried up powdered milk.

God already knows we can be a hot mess sometimes; He just wants us to recognize those conditions, and understand that the blood of Christ Jesus holds power in the remission of all our sins. The only way out of our mess is through who? JESUS.

> And they heard the voice of the Lord God walking in the garden in the cool of the day, and Adam and his wife hid themselves from the presence of the Lord God amongst the trees of the garden (Genesis 3:8 KJV).

Meaning that the Lord God does not carry the Glory, but has a presence similar of one who's in a natural state. Worship Leaders, Fasting Folks, and People who seek God's Glory understand that there are times God will instruct the covering of one's self. However, it is usually designed as spiritual guard or shield to keep out unseen spiritually things that may cause spiritual harm or hindrance while God is preserving, purifying, and healing the soul in the covering of garments. That is not the case because when God speaks, everything listens.

> Anybody who's blessed to be in God's presence knows this experience come with the fullness of joy. In God's Presence there is peace, healing, forgiveness, renewing, rebuking, wisdom, you name it. Even DEMONS have bowed and worship the Most-High (Mark 5:1-9 KJV). And the Lord God called unto Adam, and said unto him, Where art thou? (Genesis 3:9 KJV).

The Almighty God do not have to ask where His people located. God does not have to ask where art thou? God knows where you are, and He can and will meet anyone right where they at. God has eyes and hearts everywhere, and all that God has not chosen to remember is documented. It is imperative how we conduct ourselves toward humanity because every injury is reported directly back to God and He will handle it if not corrected.

> And the Lord God said unto the serpent because thou hast done this, thou art cursed above all cattle and above every beast of the field, upon thou go, and dust shalt thou eat all the days of thy life (Genesis 3:14 KJV).

God designed Humans to talk to the animals and not animals to have a full dialogue in return with the Human. One thing we know for sure that the nature of a snake is death and destruction. With a snake, no one never knows if or when a snake might strike and they are not to be used ever as pets. Snakes are always up to something deadly because it is in their nature. A snake measures and observes its victim before devouring.

Think about it, if the serpent was designed to test man and woman obedience, then why punish the serpent, if it was only doing what it designed to do? Because for years many people teach this theory that it was a test that's why the snake was punished, hogwash!

Operating with something unauthorized leads to this kind of outcome. God already knows our heart, and yes there will be tests in our life to increase one's faith building, and they are not designed to punish. God is a fair God, and He is just, and He would not have punished the serpent if that was the mission to test human's obedience. This conduct is the (Lord God) misusing ability to create. In other words, the Lord God made a monster.

Every "living thing" on earth such as humans (male or female) and varies animals, after death starts cellular deterioration in the same direction until maximal exposure which is the Skelton frame. So, what I am saying here, the Almighty GOD spoke Humans both males and females into existence all at the same time and did not need to do it from the dust of the ground manually. Everything God spoke to being was made with precision, love, and careful consideration down to each cell.

Which means everything came already packaged, including a soul; there was nothing unique about Adam being made from the dust nor the blowing of a soul living or living soul in through his nostril. However, Eve on the other hand making is unique in a questionable compacity and raises the concerns of possible incest.

The soul living wasn't something new, because God had already done it before and correctly. In the Orignal Hebrew text of Genesis Chapter 1:23 and then again in verse 30, a soul living is mention referencing animals, why? Because God wants Humans to understand that animals also have a soul living to indicate the importance of their essence or embodiment of a specified quality. Whereas, look at King James Version the soul living regarding animals is left out and published differently. See Figure 1 below:

Figure 1
Holy Bible
<u>Original Hebrew Text (First Sentence)</u>

> Translation 2 (Second Sentence)
> Translation 3 (English Text 3rd Sentence)
> Translation 4 (Right corner King James English Version)

Genesis Chapter 1

1:23	וַיְהִי	- עֶרֶב	וַיְהִי	- בֹּקֶר	יוֹם חֲמִישִׁי : פ	[23] And the evening and the morning were the fifth day.
	u·iei	- orb	u·iei	- bqr	ium chmishi : p	
	and he-is-becoming	evening	and he-is-becoming	morning	day fifth	

1:24	וַיֹּאמֶר	אֱלֹהִים תּוֹצֵא	הָאָרֶץ	נֶפֶשׁ חַיָּה	לְמִינָהּ	[24]. And God said, Let the earth bring forth the living creature after his kind, cattle, and creeping thing, and beast of the earth after his kind: and it was so.
	u·iamr	aleim thutza	e·artz	nphsh chie	l·min·e	
	and he-is-saying	Elohim she-shall-bring-forth	the earth	soul living	to species-of her	

	וְהַבְּהֵמָה	וָרֶמֶשׂ	וְחַיְתוֹ - אֶרֶץ	לְמִינָהּ	וַיְהִי	- כֵן :	
	beme u·rmsh	u·chith·u	- artz l·min·e	u·iei	- kn :		
	beast and moving anms.	and animal-of him	land to species-of her	and he-is-becoming	so		

What is the definition of a soul? Major well-known dictionaries overall description it's the spiritual or immaterial part of a human being or animal, regarded as immortal. (The key is understanding the humans have both soul and spirit which means humans have a diverse essence than of an animal).

1. A person's moral or emotional nature or sense of identity.

2. The essence or embodiment of a specified quality (Oxford Dictornary, 2017).

Side Note: Let's pause for a second and address the making of Eve from Adam's Rib and how it is viewed by some as family and not a spousal union and which brought about the possible outcomes of such practices of murder due to chromosome malfunction.

Cain killed his brother Abel, and there are suggestions that some killers are born from a family of an incest union, and due to the close sexual relation of one's family causes a chemical imbalance in the brain of that offspring. Some suggest, if that child, is then placed in a hostile environment for an extended period of time, increases the offset of that chemical imbalance of their bain. Are these hidden truths that don't get conversation simulation? Instead, other conversational norms heavily focus on things such as retardation, deformity or down syndrome when incest behavior discussed.

Genesis Chapter 2:4 demonstrates one who is mighty, but not the same as ALL Mighty, the Sufficient One. Whereas Genesis 2:4 reveals more so, an unauthorized directional evil entity who is wanting to take the place of or become like the Almighty God. Unfortunately, his results ruled out unsuccessfully, which could be why Humanity has faced and is facing such hostile experiences both physical and spiritual for centuries. This evil one wants to destroy as much of Humanity possible, if not all of Humanity's existence, especially those who practice good will and good intentions.

Please note that in the Original Hebrew Text, Genesis 2:4 uses the words genealogical annals of how Adam and Eve's lived in the Garden of Eden. Genesis 2:4 establishes the generations of Adam and their making, which also including the making of more animals, but to only reside in the Garden of Eden. Similar to Genesis Chapter 1 series of events but they are not the same incidents or outcome. The Almighty GOD sent humanity out into the Earth to live and multiply and have dominion over that which He blessed to part take of. The translation is clear between the two events, but many have smoothed out those scriptures into one event of occurrences when translation is showing otherwise. God is not limited to a garden and to get out of trapped areas in this life, change the mindset, to see the salvation of God through the Lord Jesus Christ. Spiritual Visine to see greater on a massive scale versus a restricted one.

Often I hear many Christians say let's go back to Eden.

- Are they sure, they want to go there?
- Too many things went wrong in the Garden of Eden, and I do not want to go there.

KNOW WHO YOU SERVE
(Let's Look Closer)

CHAPTER 6
KNOW WHO YOU SERVE

Genesis chapter 3 verses 22: And the <u>Lord God</u> said, Behold, the man is become as one of **us**, to know good and evil and lest he put forth his hand, and take also of the tree of life, and eat, and live forever.

Let's dissect this verse

1. And the Lord God said, Behold, the man is become as one of us.

   The above scripture is how I know even the more, that the Lord God is not same, as the Almighty GOD, because in Genesis chapter 1 verse 26:

   And God said, let us make human in our image, after our likeness (Genesis 1:26 KJV)

   Observe how the Lord God immediately started a conversation amongst the other beings with the same ability to make humans as well. Notice when the Lord God turned and said, "Behold, the man is become as one of us."

   Clearly, the Lord God did not understand God's plan from the beginning. God did not have a problem with a human having His likeness because, again God said, in Genesis chapter 1 verse 26: And God said, let us make human in our image, after our likeness. Keep in mind one of the common things The Almighty God bestowed us the ability to reproduce at all levels, but never to mismanage. Likeness: simply means the quality of being alike.

Observe closely "likeness" was approved by God earlier on and He deemed it okay to be so, but then why all of the sudden likeness was not okay from Lord God? Why?

Because two different Beings are at work here.

Lack of understanding God's blueprints, great errors occurs when trying to mimic God's Plan and it happens due to not being on one accord with God. God has already approved the likeness, but the enemy tries to stop what God has already confirmed. Let's look further:

2. To know good and evil and lest he put forth his hand,

What is wrong with knowing good and evil? By knowing so, one now has the ability to know what is good and bad for their life.

If one chooses evil, then that is that individual's fate, and the fact is he or she was aware of the good knowledge but chose it not. Often people try to dictate or control other people's life and say things such as, "Oh that's a sin," but is it a sin? Being aware of good and evil is necessary. Example: Fire is very dangerous and deadly, and it is important that we know the good and the bad of handling fire. If the fire handled correctly, it becomes a good thing such as (1) keeping warm temperature (2) cooking food (3) destroying or repairing (4) and also can be used as light etc.

However, fire can also be bad if mishandled. If someone intentionally used fire to burned down a person's home, then that is evil by the act and also a crime. So what is wrong being aware of knowing good and evil knowledge? Nothing.

3. And take also of the tree of life, and eat, and live forever.

   The above event confirmed the wick one. "The tree of life." Satan did not want the man or women to live their fullest potential nor does Satan want us to live forever. This Evil is limited, and God is unlimited and is forever. God has never put an expiration day on life only evil has. God is solid as a tree and is LIFE! Even upon death, we get a life, (now what kind of life depends on prior).

   When I read this, God said to me; I come to give life more abundantly, I sent JESUS to earth so that All Humans might have a great Life forever! Jesus took power from death and afterward God then promoted Jesus to LORDSHIP and appointed Christ Jesus as Lord or Lords, hence Jesus is now called <u>Lord Jesus</u>. "See there is increase popping up again because God is about growth."

   Based on the information I had heard from several people, I asked, God why did you negotiate with a fallen angel known as Lucifer? I just don't understand an angel, negotiating with you the Almighty God? I wanted to know what is so special about this fallen angel beside the beauty and musical ability to cause so much pain and hurt in HUMAN lives? And the answer I received was because we are up against an evil bigger than a fallen angel in which we have been lead to believe, the obvious evil one.

   Satan always sends out the assigned first before showing

up, and the whole time this information has been right there in the scriptures. Can anyone see? If so, now command the Devil to flee, for he has no power and dominion over your life, he is only pimping or trying to pimp what God already created inside you.

God said, this is why the blood and death of Jesus were called brought with a price and that the resurrection of Jesus position ALL Humans have a chance to a better life and now all souls belong to God regardless of whom created humankind. Satan wanted humanity destroyed and still does. What Satan did was he negotiated with God, only because the stats favored in the hopelessness for Humans, but God saw mercy and loved toward humanity.

Satan made the stakes high, because of the hopeless state of humanity he just knew he would win. Jesus came to earth in the natural state to live amongst humanity, but by doing so, it also put Jesus at a great risk to survive the negotiation that if Jesus died sinless, then that is the price paid that allowed all men and women to belong to God.

People, Satan does not weigh in lightly because he predicted Jesus would not accomplish such a hard task, but he was completely wrong. To know when someone is losing a fight they will try to create many distractions possible.

The Devil tried to tempt Jesus when He was fasting on the mountain, and Jesus said humans shall not live by bread alone, but by every word that proceeds from the mouth of God. The Devil did everything he possibly could through people, up until the very end to try to get Jesus to sin before He died. When that did not work, Jesus was beaten until He was almost unrecognizable and parts of His flesh hung off his body. Jesus suffered through all that pain and still did not give in. Later Jesus was nailed to the cross, and while Jesus hung there, soldiers stabled holes in His side with a sword and wounded Jesus.

As Jesus hung on the cross for hours, they offered Jesus vinegar, instead of water to drink to quench His thirst, and still, Jesus hung there for Humanity and died for all our sins. Christ Jesus paid the price for our sins. Thank You, JESUS! People, please understand what is against your success and call upon the true and living Almighty GOD through Christ Jesus for help. We have authority to cast Satan down, out of our family, out of our finances, and out of our life. Amen Hallelujah Glory be to God.

Satan wants to keep us bound and trapped living boxed in somewhere. Why live that way? When God has given us a whole big earth to subdue. For many years the wick ones have tried to use the Holy Bible to keep People bound by their made up standards, but what ended up happening is the Holy Bible freed many who were spiritually captive.

The enemies were handling something great (the Holy Bible) but just did not know how great. People everywhere we do not have to wait on large corporations to give us jobs, they operate because humanity works for them. They exist because you exist and they need you just as much as you need them.

And Women, please do not think for another second that you are lesser because God made female at the same time he made a male. Some of the most wonderful people I have ever met were Women.

Unfortunately, there have been and still are several forms of evil (including certain types of women), for years who have tried to trap women to believe the untruth they are the ones that caused humanity to fall, my beloved that too is a lie!!!

What a cruel form of control, but Women guess what, God has given you the power to rebuke those lies and God will have your back in the process. Please keep standing People of God don't give up and by all means don't let go. All things are possible through Christ Jesus, our liaison.

Now my question to the Readers is:

Understand who Satan is? God has given this great revelation, now speak to the Satan with authority and denounce him through CHRIST JESUS.

GET OUT OF THE GARDEN OF EDEN!

There's nothing good there in that garden

To get out of trapped areas in life, change the mindset

Faith Believers regardless of ethnicity start building, start owning, subdue the earth and all its riches. Contrary to what's said amongst the corrupt ones nor what it looks like or the challenges happening right now. God Do not have respectable persons, He can bless you too. God will Make room for you! Start a business, obtain ownership of properties, and work together with ethical people who will build apartment communities and housing that do not take advantage of Humanity.

What the greedy owners are doing to us is no longer a business for profit, but it is greed and over-assessing in its purest form. If generations before lived off less and still made it with a good life. Certainly, the resources available now, our life should be greater and not struggle. No longer pay $1100-$1800 a month for a small one-bedroom apartment, because this kind of living or lifestyle does not promote ownership, nor does it promote independence.

What happens in this financial state of being, is the cost of living experience capture one's whole paycheck, and many find themselves never saving enough money that will overall benefit the essence of substantial saving. That is just where the system design wants us to remain in a state of poverty and not profit. Skillfully designed that even after the age 30 a roommate is needed and just so you know, it is a fancy form of welfare assistance. How? Because someone's help is needed in order to afford housing.

After conducting an analysis, my findings show that Urban Planning and Infrastructure Management across the board does not promote true ownership and independence to the status quo of ordinary working-class persons in the major urban cities here in America. Whereas the illusion of ownership created on paper, but truth is the marketing drives promote and forcibly pushes this generation always to be found in a leasing status or never actually fully owning their property, and until it is paid off, it is not yours. Wait!

Even then once paid, some mandates set in place that could very well take the owner out of ownership status. If one tried to own a condo the monthly maintenance fees alone are very expensive so bottom line you don't own it.

Many people are tricked and betrayed by the hype of buying it and flipping it. Whereas, due to the highs and lows of the housing market, that method gets old very fast. Most of all it can become very unethical and corrupt if mishandled because most housing asking price is not even close to the requested value. Example: Some houses at best cost $35, 000, then someone buys it, and fix it up "somewhat" then sell it for $450,000? That is not Kingdom Building, and that is not the mind of God, for humanity, but that is "Theft"!

Keep in mind most buying and flipping practices is not designed for people who do not have extra money or income already. Property owners or investors get away with this greed because the people no longer create a standard in legislation nor do enough people fight for their consumer's rights. This kind of Real Estate Practices has absolutely nothing to do with the times we are living in, and this type of greed should no longer be excused. Not to mention, if not ethically careful, "flipping houses" could promote how to become a "Professional Realtor Thief."

Research how much the actual cost of the desired raw materials used to build the choice home. The benefits of knowing the overhead cost versus going in leaving everything solely to a construction company. Hands on is an excellent method for future home buyers to rethink their purchasing power. Don't fall victim to these errors, that so many people have due to finally deciding to take action after the "Wolf" has done a considerable amount of damage to their survivorhood and livelihood of home ownership. Invest valuable time in the available financial literature, because the image of homeownership has become a priority and not the actual investments. Many people are willing to pay $450,000 for a house built right next to an active railroad track or an open pass loud freeway that's financed with a 30-year term totaling $750,000.

Well the logical outcome, fast forward, is the elderly end up working longer because he or she mismanaged their financial youth. When all it would have taken was the simplest things to avoid future financial hardship at old age, and that was fight for your constitutional rights today. Many are nearly 70 years old and are still working not by choice. This age group should be working because of choice; American People we must do better in this generation and start working together and not divided due to greed.

I know adversaries creates an illusion that trying to own something is a long, difficult process, but the truth is, it's easier than one could imagine. If the work is put in, along with good capital (money), find a target market along with an effective Business Plan, and connection with the right people then ownership is within reach to start that business.

※

God has many educated individuals who went to business school, and they know what I am saying is true. The thing is a vast majority of Universities in America focus on operations more and maybe a little on practice depending on the Professor who is teaching that business course. I am yet to find a University that teaches OWNERSHIP, and Practice. Operational Education can get someone a job, but that only positions a person to always work for somebody else and there's nothing wrong with that.

Let's change the world's view about Godly People and Prosperity. Recap the previous information written regarding a starting pointing to greater wealth in this climate change here in America.

If appropriate economic infrastructures built with truly affordable housing in mind while producing apartment communities with reasonable leasing rates, the people would move in those establishments. Overnight, many would move-out those over-priced prisons called apartments, lofts, and condos that overall underneath the surface is never actually owned.

We must break this generational financial curse, for the well-being of Humanity. Nothing fabulous about living paycheck to paycheck or having a roommate(s) to survive the high rent cost, nor is it worth it, to take away hard-earned income, just to say you live in that overpriced community. Nothing fabulous about always being financially broke or living on a strict budget, NO MY FRIENDS, these examples are not a good living. Overpriced housing owners are not concerned about the livelihood and well-being of their tenants, but only interest is the increase in their already fat bank accounts at your expense. We have the power to create NO! We have the power to create NO! We have the power to create NO! We have the power to create NO! Powerful Together end of story.

People everywhere learn about Urban Planning and learn the laws and regulations in your city, and your state; along with our federal laws governed to protect us as the people and guess what, these regulations are public access and having a law degree is not required to understand your rights.

Get the knowledge, that way when the devil comes, and he will, start speaking the law and rebuke the devour and BUILD for the sake of this generation!!! God gave authority, so use it, and position back what God originally purpose for Life, Love, and Liberty. By all means, be mindful of people who will try to tailor God to their limitations.

People of God, always move in facts confirmed by the wisdom

of God. Often people get the facts and change them or merge the truth all into one, and that can be misleading, and damaging, and it causes many generations lost in the wilderness for years, and in some cases, perish from the lack of knowledge. Please note there is more than one evil being, but often the obvious evils are solely reviewed and called all as the same. But Beloved they are not all the same, for there are different kinds of evil dressed in many forms. God has given Humanity the power and authority to take back their life and live abundantly.

*"The Garden of Eden
Failed Humanity
But We don't have too."*

~Nitoric Jenkins~

*Thank You for Reading
Be Blessed*

Check Points

- ✓ Sunday's school lessons are not enough studying.
- ✓ Studying requires "RESEARCH" from credible sources, along with the Bible.
- ✓ Many have for years are teaching off what someone else said be doctrine, and quoting things that have no validity to an act of SIN or being sinful.
- ✓ From time to time measure a correlation between your Life's Successes and your Faith.
- ✓ A Saved Holy Ghost Filled Life: Should also equal Relationship, Research, and Questions.
- ✓ Stop getting up there teaching people if you have researched NOTHING.
- ✓ In other words, stop (pimping) the church just to have an INCOME!!! Are you working in the church because of relationship and service, or profit? If the money stop would you still be there?

Lastly,

- ✓ When the leaders have no vision, therefore their members will not either. However, my prayers are with the ones who do step out of the box.
- ✓ Deep Folks in the church is always talking about wanting something "new" in God, well there now.

People Are Hurting

People are hurting in the church and outside the church and need answers for life's journeys, and so when they assemble themselves in the house of God that is in Christ Jesus. Whereas, once inside the Sanctuary, often today they encounter Fake, Self-Absorbed, Bi-Polar, and Money Pimping Church People and Leaders. So, then these hurting individuals leave that church service still hurting, more confused with no plans of ever coming back, or struggling to come back to church because they cannot tell the difference between the delivered and ethical church leaders. Valid reasons as to why the church has lost real anointed power or never had it in the first place, while many are left wondering why "the world" is looking at their ministries with a side eye.

Spiritual Traps

Here are some of the problems why faith-based believers are struggling and are financially broke and limited to accessible wealth that is literally within reach. Many church folks use the scriptures "be in the world but not of the world." That does not mean go section off somewhere in the corner of the earth or only hang around people who only agree with your beliefs. Understand the difference in cultures, core values, and beliefs; instead of generalizing everything to salvation.

Some Christians say they don't want to hang around those people, they might cause them to do wrong, well maybe that kind of Christians may just need little more Jesus. Don't mix up "the world," with past "fetishes," because not everybody intentions are fowl. Go in and revolutionize by showing "the world" you are a person walking in integrity, one who operates in absolutely no hidden motives, while projecting excellent business ethics. One who raises the banner that demonstrates it is perfectly okay, to do the right thing always, and project that yes morale still exists. Increase the volume that yes Christians are educated, yes many are skilled and smart enough to manage and function successfully in Leadership Roles without turning every moment or conversation into a church service.

Stop trying to turn the workplace into a personal worship center or promoting every conversation church-related, with passive-aggressive judgment and condemnation. (Many single folks wonder why they are yet single, it could be because that would have been spouse was not trying to sign on for all of their intimate interactions to be a church moment). Understand a lifestyle lived implements consistent professional character, and reflexes like the sun and encounters will know there is a difference about the character that's before them.

The world needs to see, oh wow they had clean fun, oh wow they came together and did not have a fight, oh wow they have integrity toward one another. If the church does not embrace the world at some point, then who's fought is it when on a job, and you are the only person of faith hired on, or you got a Devil for Manager, while each day you at war in the parking lot debating if should you go back inside. God wants us to live life abundantly, and by all means make sure your ministry does not come off as a cult, but rather a place of faith, healing, and worship.

War Inside the Camp

So many Leaders in the church who are preaching did not get a formal education, nor has any intentions of getting any form of higher learning that will help further their teaching effectiveness.

What happens is that kind of church Leader has a settle verbal and vicious form of attack against their members who have gotten an education or has premier income. Of course, many pretend they are glad for their member's success but their actions are bitter, and the heart seems dark. The reality is, no more excuses trying to justify churches' lack today, by referencing back to the worship experiences of the old Leaders from 100 years ago. Because we as people of intelligence know that the older generation did not have educational opportunities and many things they just did not know or was cautious to accept.

However, God gave those Leaders and People a magnitude of wisdom, and that is the difference versus some of the Leadership practices today; many of these Leaders don't have the wisdom to move effectively in God's Kingdom. Such Leaders desperately need and want a form of "superior identity" or some glorified self-worth and especially if they are not or were not successful in everyday strives toward gainful employment, and of course, in their ill mind, the next closest thing to prestige is having a leadership role in the Church.

Because after all it is a good look to be in church leading, but the truth is, that recognition only belongs to heart changed People of God through Christ Jesus, individuals who will handle and operate from divine instructions so that God's work may go forth efficiently. Unfortunately, and sadly, those lost Leaders are easily spotted because he or she always wants everyone to know their title and that they are a Preacher, Missionary, Evangelist, Elder, Pastor, or a Bishop. The reality is no one cares, except that individual who is self-promoting themselves. What people overall concern is the life-changing experience and edification projected representing Kingdom Building.

Sincere demeanor does not need validation from others because they have the true evidence flowing within and in their daily walk so they don't have to feel the need to tell anyone who they are because it will come shining out like the sun.

Disorder Leadership

Hmm, what's up with this? Some people are coming to a Holy place dressed like they are headed to the strip club or just left the strip club, and this raises eyebrows, especially those individuals who are up 'ministering" to people. Is this a huge sign no Holy Ghost is dwelling on the inside? Because being filled makes one aware and positions him or her before the Holy of Holies, meaning it is no longer desired to stand before God's presence looking and acting any ole kind of way, and this method also applies to after church service attire. Of course, one can override the atmosphere and operate in disobedience, but it is hazardous overall for one's soul to do so.

Can someone be in God authentically, ministering and preaching to people dressed as a prostitute, or looking like something hustling on the streets? The Men in oversized clothes, butt hanging out clothes, slagging clothes, strange signs, and symbols that demonstrate possible gang relation or mimicked street's body language and behavior. There has to be a divine difference in approach and the reasons many people who try to superimposed this madness and don't understand or get frustrated as to why the church resists, it's because Jesus changed them once from being that hustling person, so it isn't anything new. Don't get fooled by the cheerleaders and supporters approving this malfunction. Oh, so the reasoning for this kind of behavior, is ministers are trying to reach a particular type of young people, right? Lie! God's word has enough convicting power to reach any person, and He does not need an illusion of His power, the question is their authorization to deliver because God can reach the heart of anyone right where they are, through Christ Jesus. Whereas, to fully know this Kingdom's information is to have experienced it.

Some women ministers are up preaching in these ridiculous (woman of the night) extra high-heeled shoes, hair all kinds of odd colors, teeth pimped out, skin inked out, and breast popped out and up. All while having the nerves to look down on the guys who wear sagging pants showing underwear and butt print and suggesting for them to pull their pants, (which they should pull their pants up), the double standard is yet their whole breast is showing all but the nipple. I suggest cover that up too because that is not freedom of a fashion expression, but a publicized rated X version of one's self. SMH so lost. If money was found to put it on the body, well find money to clean it off before leading anybody. More importantly, wouldn't Holy Ghost filled people cover themselves, but the undelivered will not and the un-called ministers will then try to justify it's a modern world style or taste (Lie!). All while trying to shut-up Saintly people who have a long-standing effective ministry.

There is no correlation between the two because looking good is one thing, mishandle God's convicting image is another. Well if anyone is upset at this point, just know it is only the seductive things still dwelling within. The heart always reveals what's going on inside, and just because no one says anything about that conduct, does not mean it's not regularly viewed as questionable by the people near and far.

Keeping the integrity of God's word clean and pure, so when someone seeks for answers or search for change, clear direction is available, in hopes of restoration. A path that will ensure those individuals will part take in uncontaminated ministry for efforts toward wholeness.

Leaders in Ministry for Years, Pimping isn't easy hmm

How can Leaders be effective when they don't have any structure themselves, perhaps hiding behind the big-name title says otherwise? A Preacher once called a group of people common, yet their reflection screamed basic, having not once impact humanity into greater shift. Traveling and Preaching at church to church does not make one great nor does being loud make one be in yoke breaking mode because if there is no anointing power, does not matter how loud one sound, nothing going to change or shift in the spiritual atmosphere. Some Pastors and Leaders have been ministering for 5-60 years have never put up a professional Church Sign at their church. Yet, every year, anniversary money is collected, their first lady has never worn the same expensive hat twice, new suits for both regularly, new car every other year, tithes & offerings paid by members, but no church sign or enough restrooms to accommodate the people or guests. Then those Pastors will get upset when someone gets up and go to the rest because their ill leadership and mismanagement can't comprehend the error because after all, no one can tell them anything nor can their self-absorption see past having only one restroom per gender is poor management. If Walmart, Target, and other places all have a sign, don't you think it's wise to have one as well, so the people can know what the ministry is about before entering. In this season, God is separating the Wheat from Weeds and exposing this eroded lack.

Whereas, go to their home or personal living space, and witness these individuals will not accept anything less than 2-3 restrooms. Then when they think they are doing something great in ministry, they go out and purchase with the church's money or collected money from the church and buy these very expensive Preacher's Apparel. In other words, clown suits, or stage performance costumes, I look at it like this, if it can not be worn every single day, then it has no validity confirming salvation or establishing a correlation to being Holy. All it is, is show and tell or symbolic at best and not required. Because in Christ Jesus, no matter what level, title, or role any believer has, there is absolutely NO IMPRISONMENT in Christ Jesus, but complete liberty. In other words, stop clowning GOD's Kingdom with your drag show, and don't try to justify with scripture about someone else's mantle mentioned in the Bible. Be a life changer versus all the symbolism and focus on a shift toward greater good within humanity; by all means, get over Self.

AUTHOR'S THOUGHTS

Eden Botched Humanity Wheat or Weeds, has truly blessed my soul, and after writing it, there was a shift in my spirit and then a spiritual uplifting of a renewed mind. As I began to praise and thank God through Christ Jesus, I realized that over time I had taken on a religious mindset, instead of the Kingdom of God mindset that first given unto me by God.

I understood God forgives if one asked, but I stop seeing God as merciful forgiver who just simply want all of us to be the best possible persons representing all His splendor.

Also, I was hard on myself, applying human-made standards and before I knew it, people ideas of what I should be like, contaminated my very essence, but never again. Just remember wick individuals and wick things will always show up trying to steal and devour what God has already done for us.

Readers, if you find my literature enjoyable, please visit my website below, and click the donation button to help support upcoming work, Thanks.

Edenbotchedhumanity.com

ABOUT THE AUTHOR

Nitoric Jenkins, a Texas native born in Dallas and later moved to northern Louisiana, where he raised by Helen Wilbert-Jenkins, Grandmother. Nitoric does not mind being transparent and stands firmly on the promises of God. At one point, Nitoric became homeless and lived in a homeless shelter during his undergraduate year of college, that experience prompted him to create a humanitarian program. As part of his charities, he created a nonprofit program called BE Empowered. A service that was rendered to the homeless in the city of Houston, particularly for residents who were in transitional housing programs.

All capital came from Nitoric's finances, and he admits there were times he needed his money for college expenses. Instead, Nitoric donated his money to the homeless toward quality food, gift cards for hygienic maintenance, direct monetary contributions, and taught free life skill classes that consisted of basic computer skills and software from his laptop. In future, Nitoric will apply for a 501c while campaigning to open an Affordable Living Apartment Community Building, a strategic goal that will help a percentage of people off to a great start.

Dr. Nitoric Jenkins earned degrees are Doctor of Education in Ethical Leadership, Master of Public Administration, and Bachelor of Business Administration in Management. When Dr. Jenkins is not contributing to help make the world a brighter place, he is off living his best life.

Acknowledgements

GRANDMOTHER HELEN (AKA NANA)

I had to stop and say Thank You

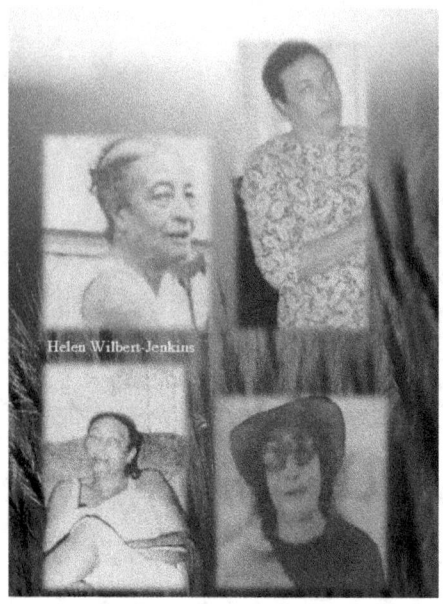
Helen Wilbert-Jenkins

If I could possibly dine with my Grandmother one last time, I would tell her Girl, Thank You! Why? Because, she was my best friend and had my back all the way, and shared her wisdom with me and invested her time freely. Helen made sure I understood the value of education and character building.

Often my Grandmother said, "all I got was a 3rd-grade education because I had to stop going to school and help my Dad chop and pick cotton. I believe in you, so please make something out of yourself. Course it is your choice to go to college, but for now, let me show how to work our vegetable gardens."

Earlier on, Helen began to teach me, several effective principals, to be a successful individual and simply learn how to provide for my family one day. One example of many, was she would take me to our large vegetable gardens after the harvest (some evenings and weekends and I will not scream it was always a sunshine experience LOL).

However, as the years proceeded and maturity set in, I had an aha moment, one day standing behind my Grandmother's screened door of our porch. My mindset changed, and I became aware and understood what was happening. I implemented the value of what being a provider meant and that if I want something, I had to work to obtain it, and it was in those moments that accompanied the building of my character, along with honesty, and integrity first hand.

Even though my Grandmother Helen had what was considered a 3rd-grade education, her wisdom made up for any lack. Helen was advance and whatever was not obtained in an Educational System(s) or setting I believed God still touched Helen's mind and our family survived.

I write this love letter in honor of my Grandmother Helen because I had to stop and say, Thanks, Nana! And to the readers of this love letter perhaps this testament will encourage and lift the head of any individuals who may be experiencing the loss of a loved one. I pray that each person grieving to please hold on and hang on in there, for the sun will shine again. God, I thank you for Christ Jesus, and for taking the pain out of the hurt Amen!

Sorrow
Now Sunshine
Helen Wilbert-Jenkins 1931-2006

Grandma Helen, the tall one standing with her Mother, Great Grandma Nodie after church.

"Real tears once busted is the medicine that calms an aching heart and soul."

~Nitoric Jenkins~

May my testament be of help to the broken-hearted who is grieving that you may find wholeness again. One week and three days before it happened I was driving home from a long day, and God gently spoke to me and said, "I am asking for her." I immediately knew who He was asking for. I began to cry and plead, "God, please do not take my best friend away from me. For I love her so and she's all I have who loves me no matter what".

So I shook off my worries and proceeded home to my apartment, and I continued my daily functions. The following week I called her local flower shop and had flowers delivered to Helen, and I felt great. A few days later I got home from a long day, threw some hot wings in the oven, and started cleaning around my apartment, and then in a sweet voice, I heard say, lay your eyes upon her, for I am asking for her.

I dropped everything I was doing, and my heart pleaded, please don't take my Grandmother from me. I packed my suitcases and didn't even care if the clothes were folded or not. I threw them into my luggage, turned off the stove, got in my car and drove. While I drove to see Nana, God continued to speak to me and told me several things that prepared me to handle what was about to happen. God reminded me of the prayers I prayed when I was a young boy.

Once I arrived, my Grandmother's world lit up as well as mines. We talked and laughed as she tried to eat the fried liver I had brought from the local chicken stand, but her appetite was low. While I was there, she raised out of her bed and said let me show you something. Helen got out of bed and walked to her wheelchair. Please understand her Doctor said, she was not going to walk again.

However, my prayers were that I might see Helen walk again, and so I prayed about it. As time went by, I forgot about that prayer, and when I witness her walking again, at that moment, my senses did not fully capture what was happening till much later. She climbed back into her bed, and we talked some more, and I said, "Nana I love you so much, and you mean everything to me." As I kissed her forehead and cheek and she said, "thank you, and I love you too," next, I placed the blankets on her legs, they were so cold to the touch, my heart dropped, and my stomach tighten because of that reality check.

❧

I tried my best to warm her feet and legs but there was no change the in the temperature, and they remained cold. Helen then said, "Death is a hard pill to swallow, but we have to go." I began to sing to her, followed by an intense prayer softly. I did not notice while I prayed, but later my cousin, Rita who was present stated, while I was praying she put her hand out for the God's help.

As I left out of her room so that she could get some rest, slowly I walked toward the door and laid my eyes on her, and I said, "Nana I love you." She said, I love you too, and the next day late that evening she closed her eyes for the last time. I whispered into her ear, and I said, Helen, please talk to the Jesus for He can hear your thoughts and I said to her for the very last time, Helen I love you and she moved her jaw and softly said I love you too.

Three days went by with little sound, and on the third night the Nurse allowed me to stay in the room the whole night, I knew that was a bad sign. That Saturday morning around 6 AM, the nurse entered the room, and Helen's vital signs dropped rapidly, and her body began to raise upright. However, in mid-air, the movement stopped, and Helen left here. As a young child, my prayer was if my Grandmother were ever to die, God, please let me be right by her side and that too came to pass.

"When I think of my Grandmother Helen, along with all the wonderful memories, it feels like I own pure gold, and that God gave me one of His most precious rare treasures. And because of this Love, each thought gets sweeter. I am honored to be a part of the Wilbert's Family Blood Line. Thank You, God, for my Grandmother! For I am Forever Grateful".

Nitoric Jenkins
(aka Hot Rod)

www.ingramcontent.com/pod-product-compliance
Lightning Source LLC
Chambersburg PA
CBHW072050290426
44110CB00014B/1620